AF394452

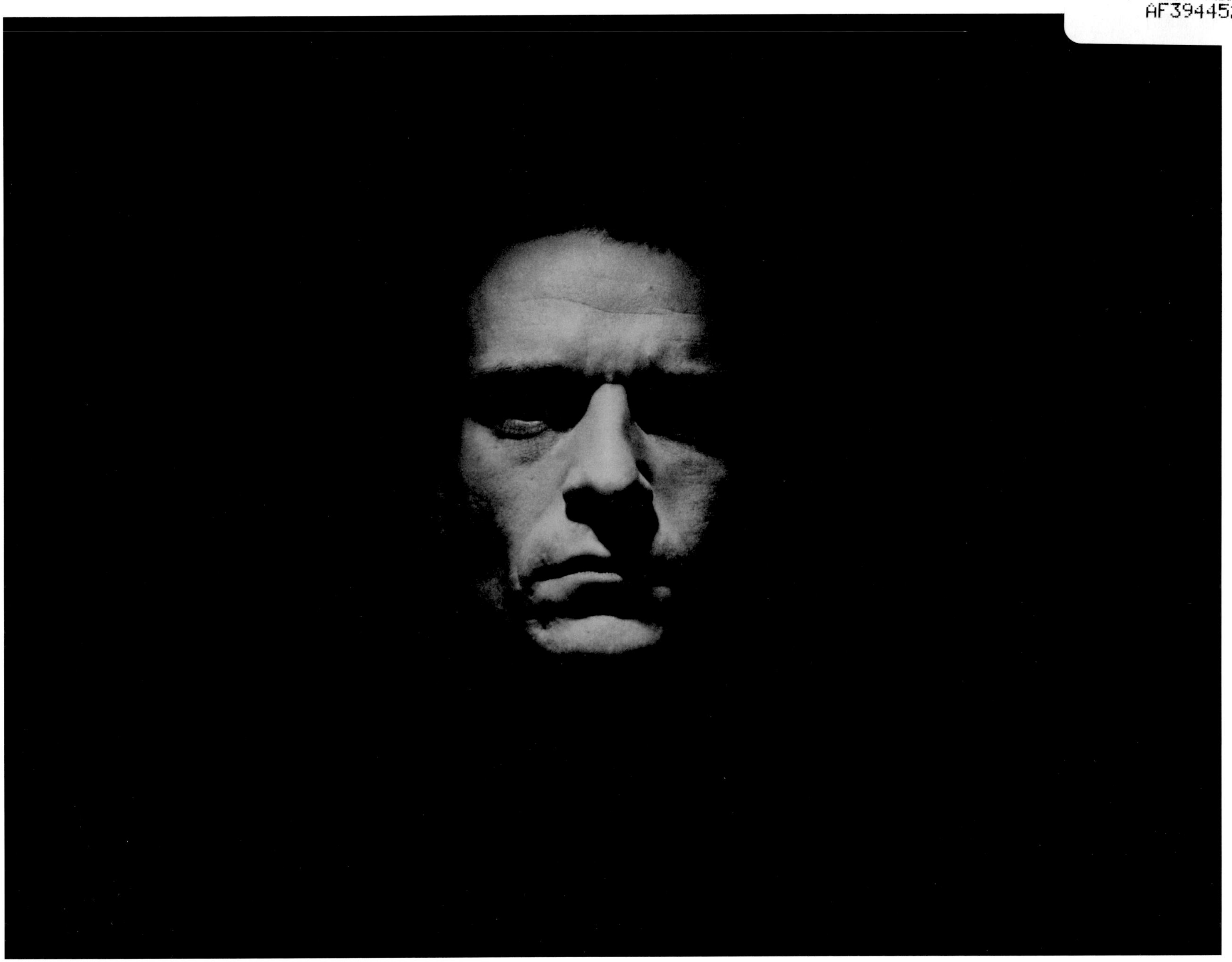

PERSONA 1012351

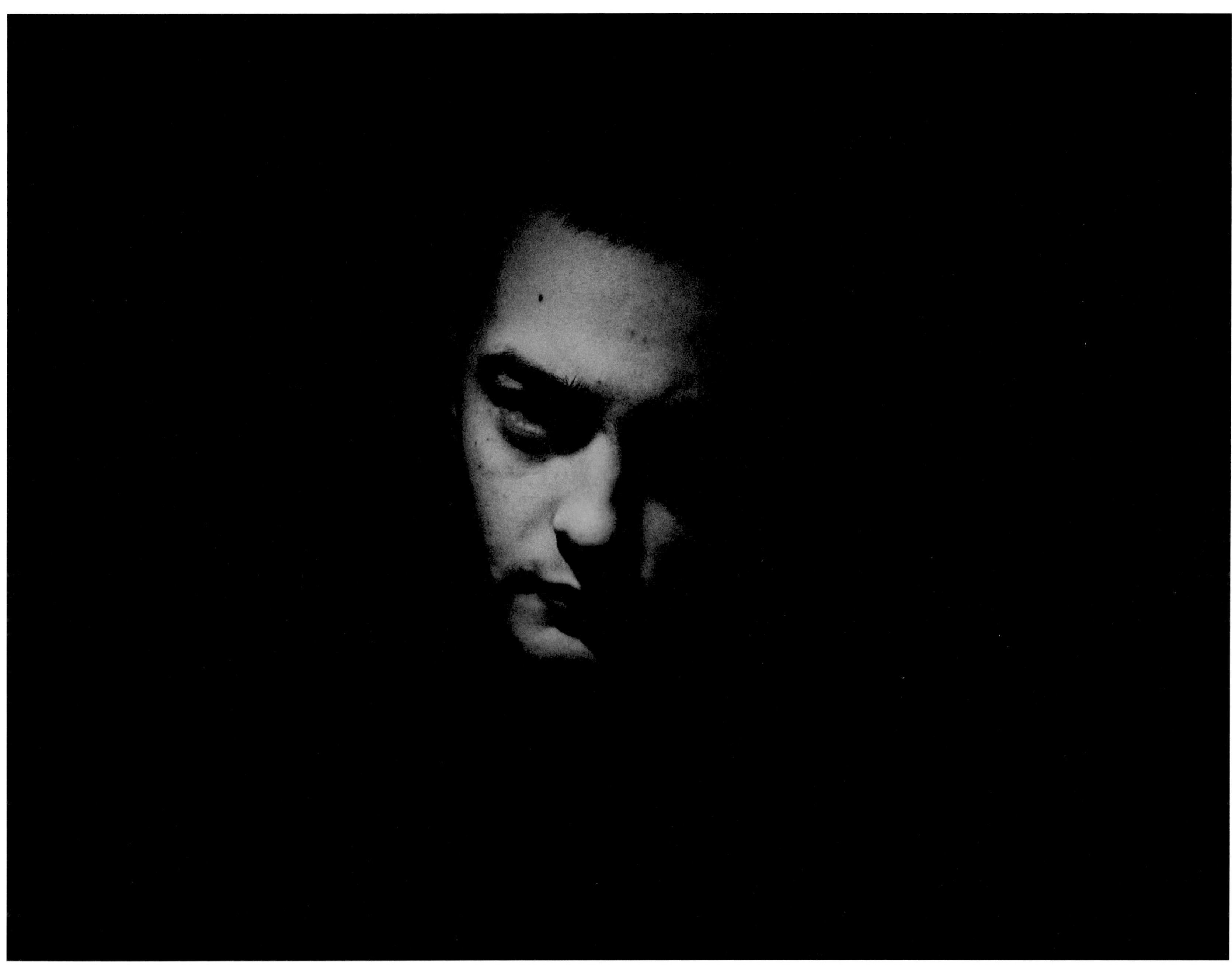

PERSONA 1019726

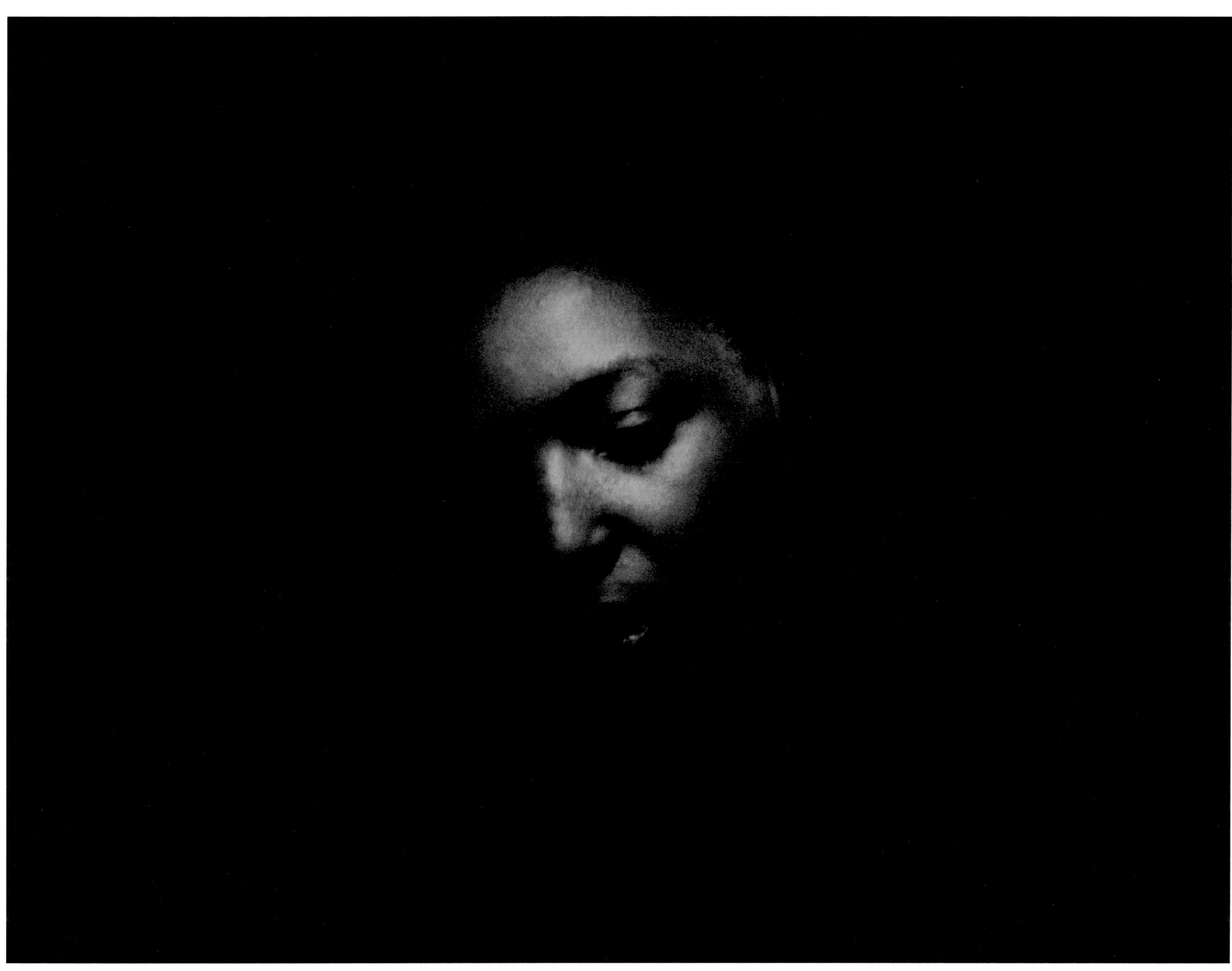

PERSONA 1018202

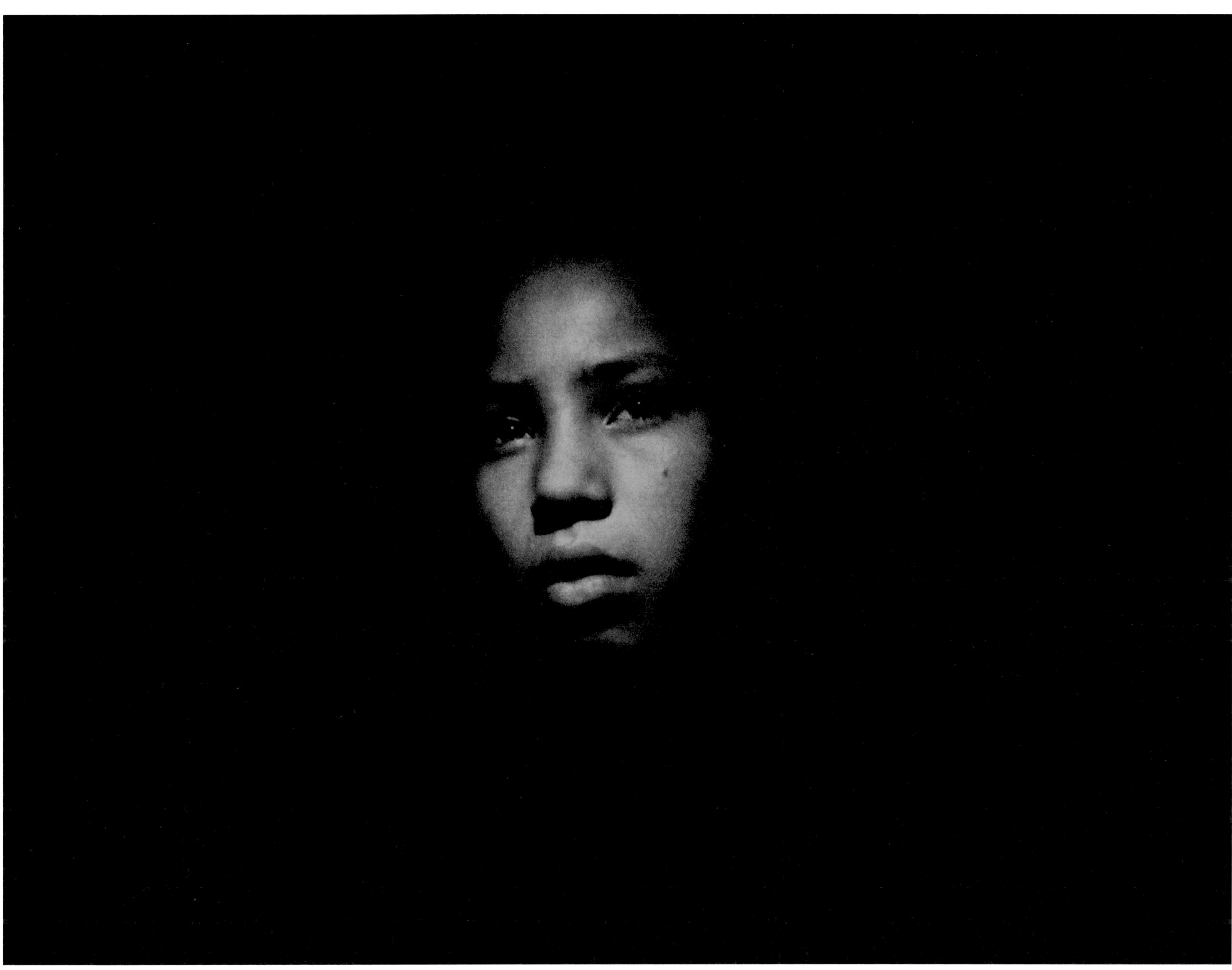

PERSONA 1010846

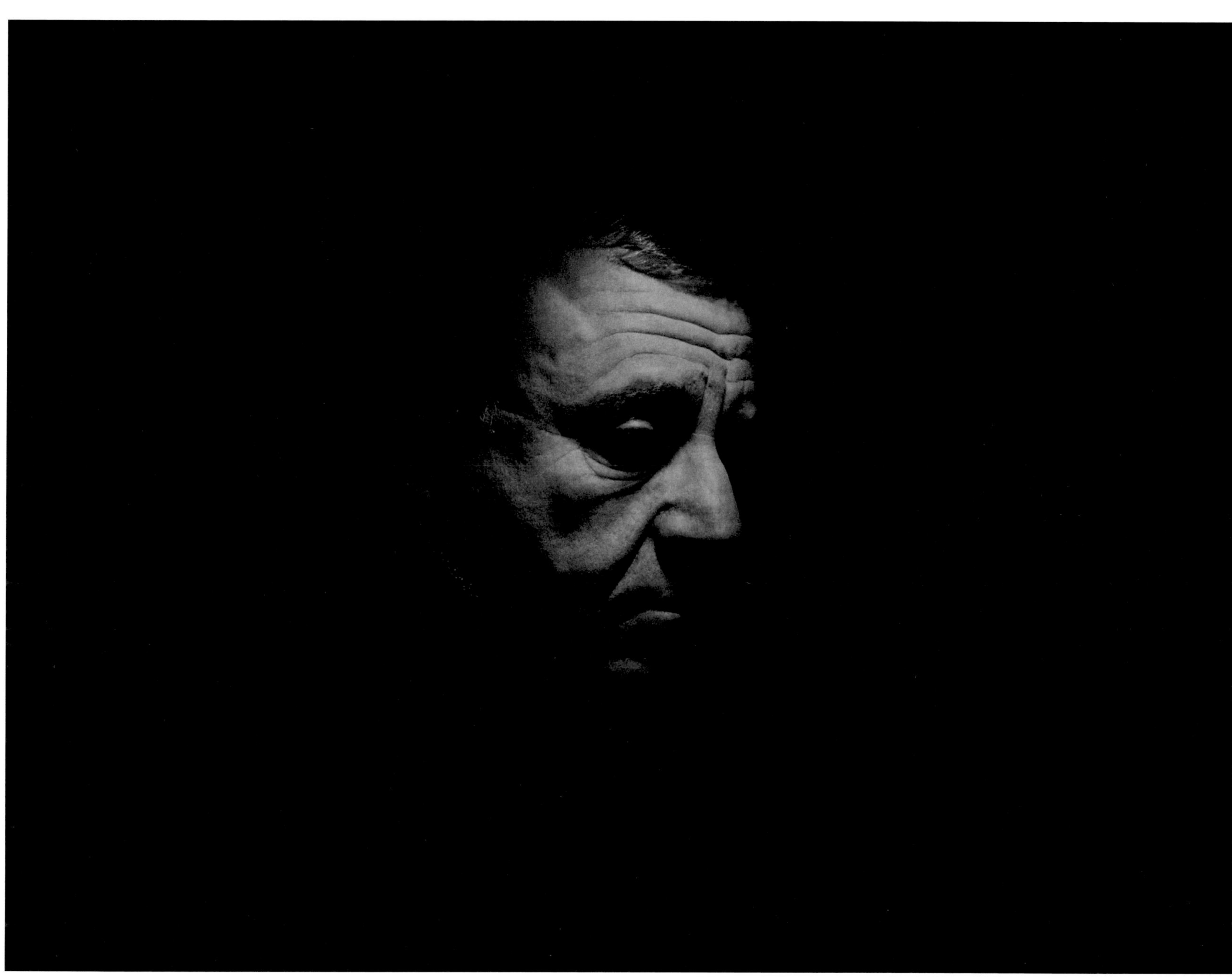

PERSONA 1011800

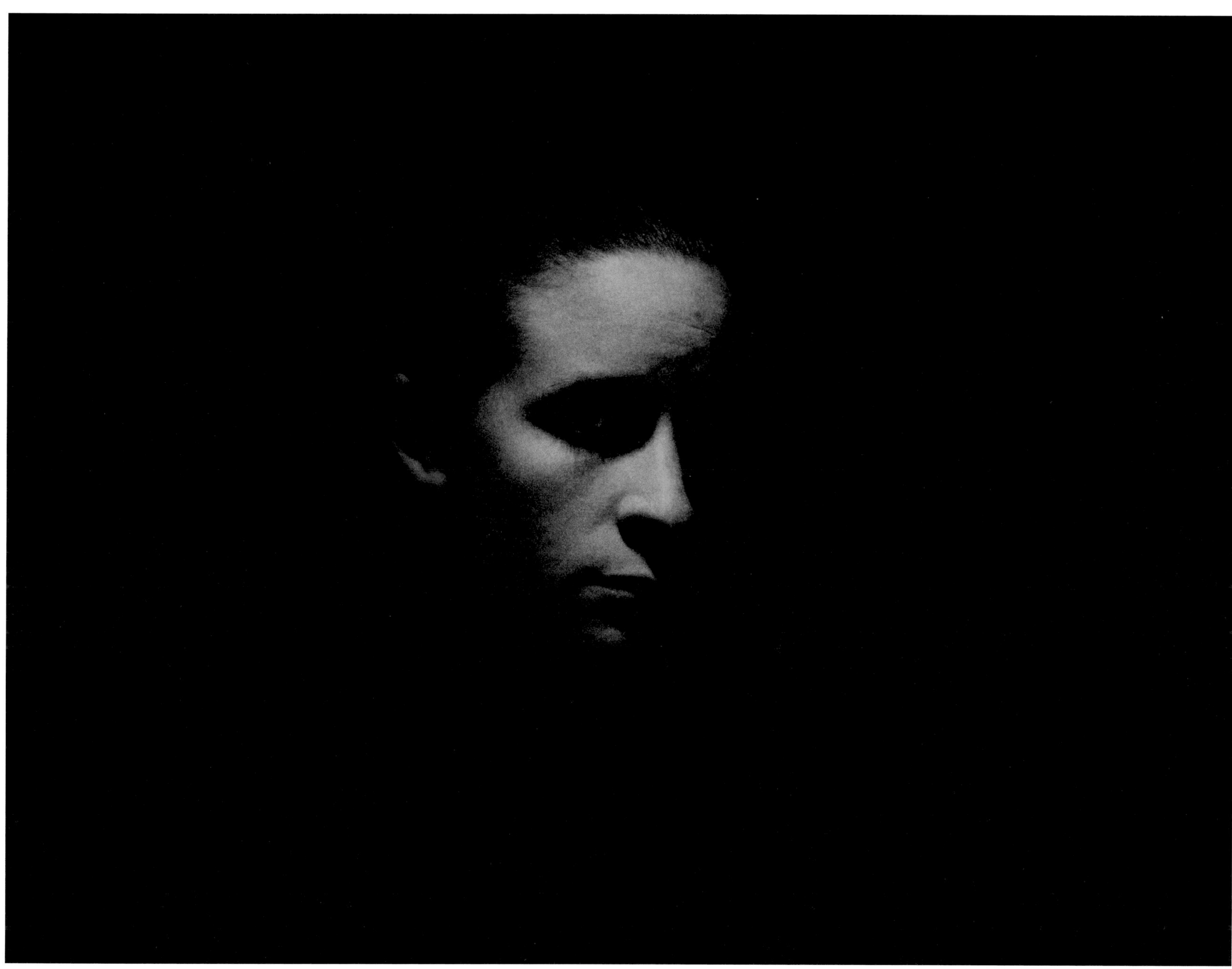

PERSONA 1018240

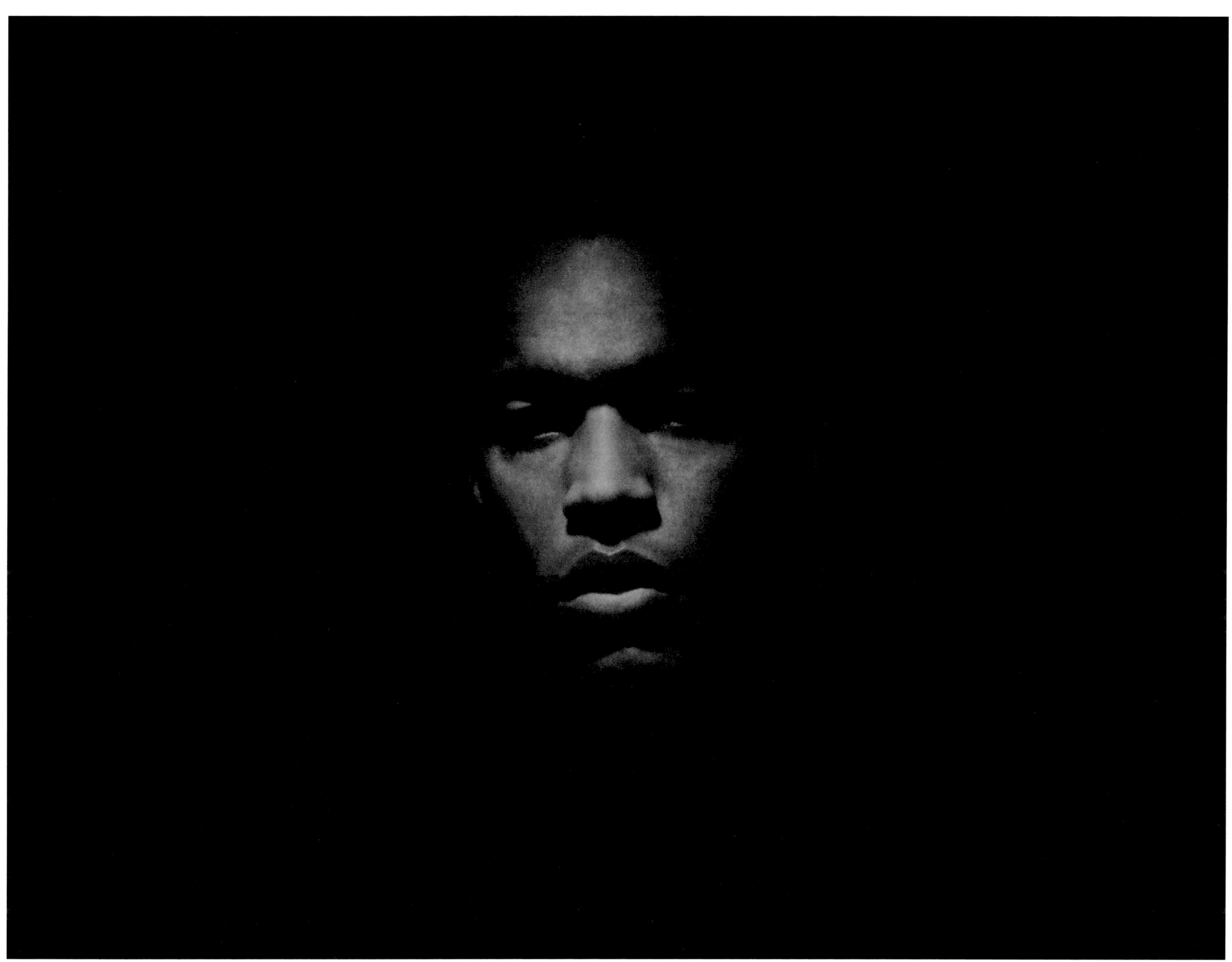

PERSONA 1011021

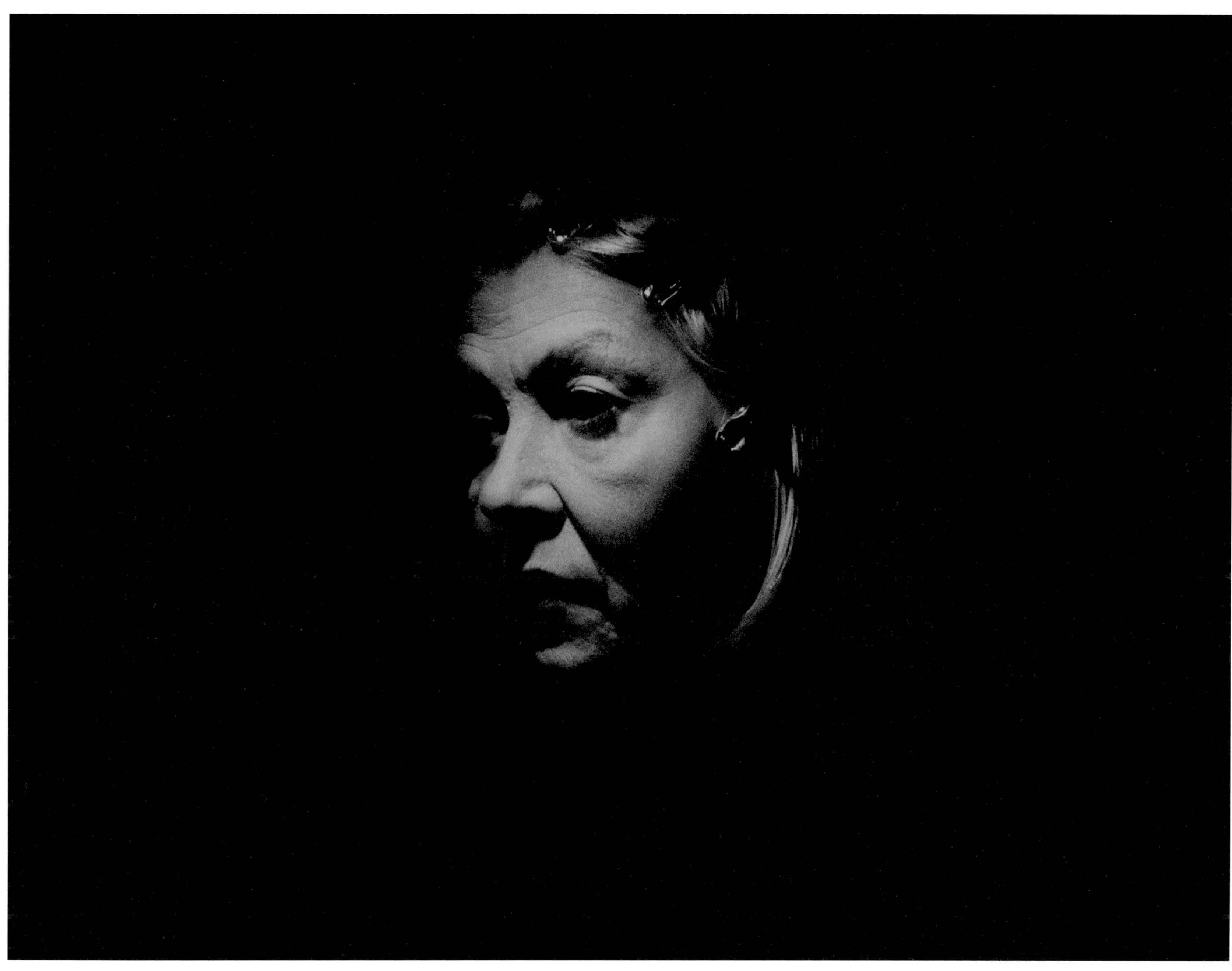

PERSONA 9102803

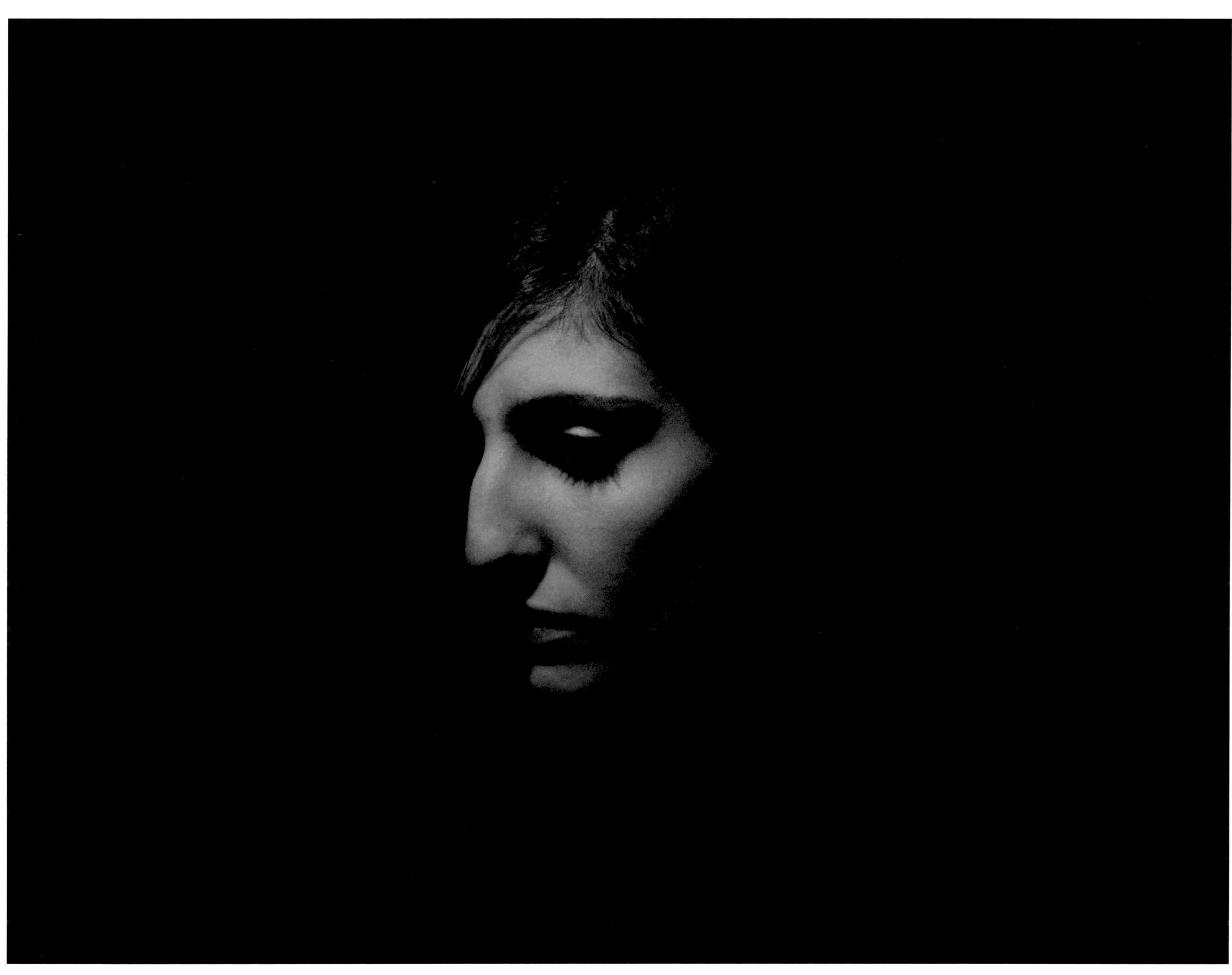

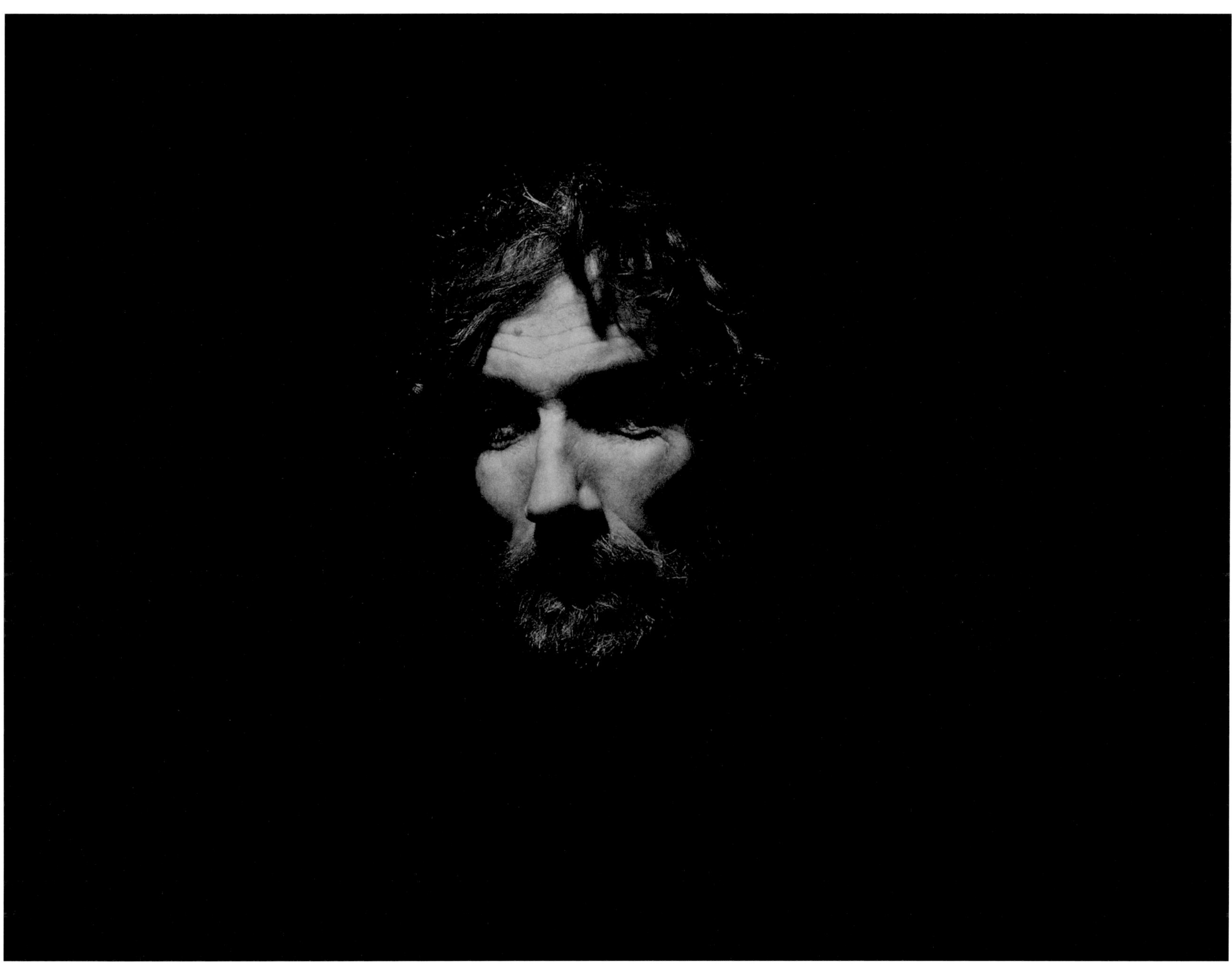

PERSONA 1018773

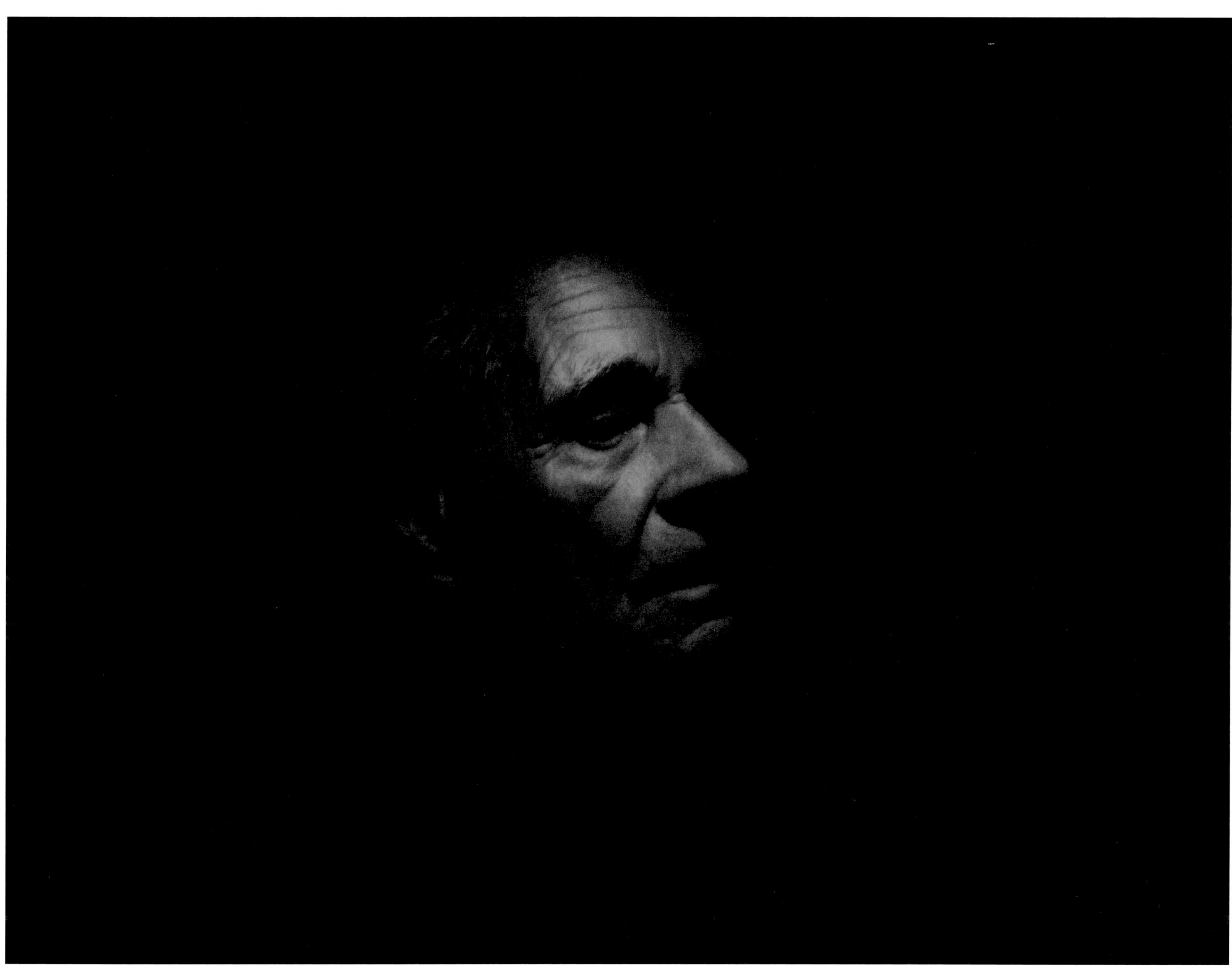

PERSONA 1015048

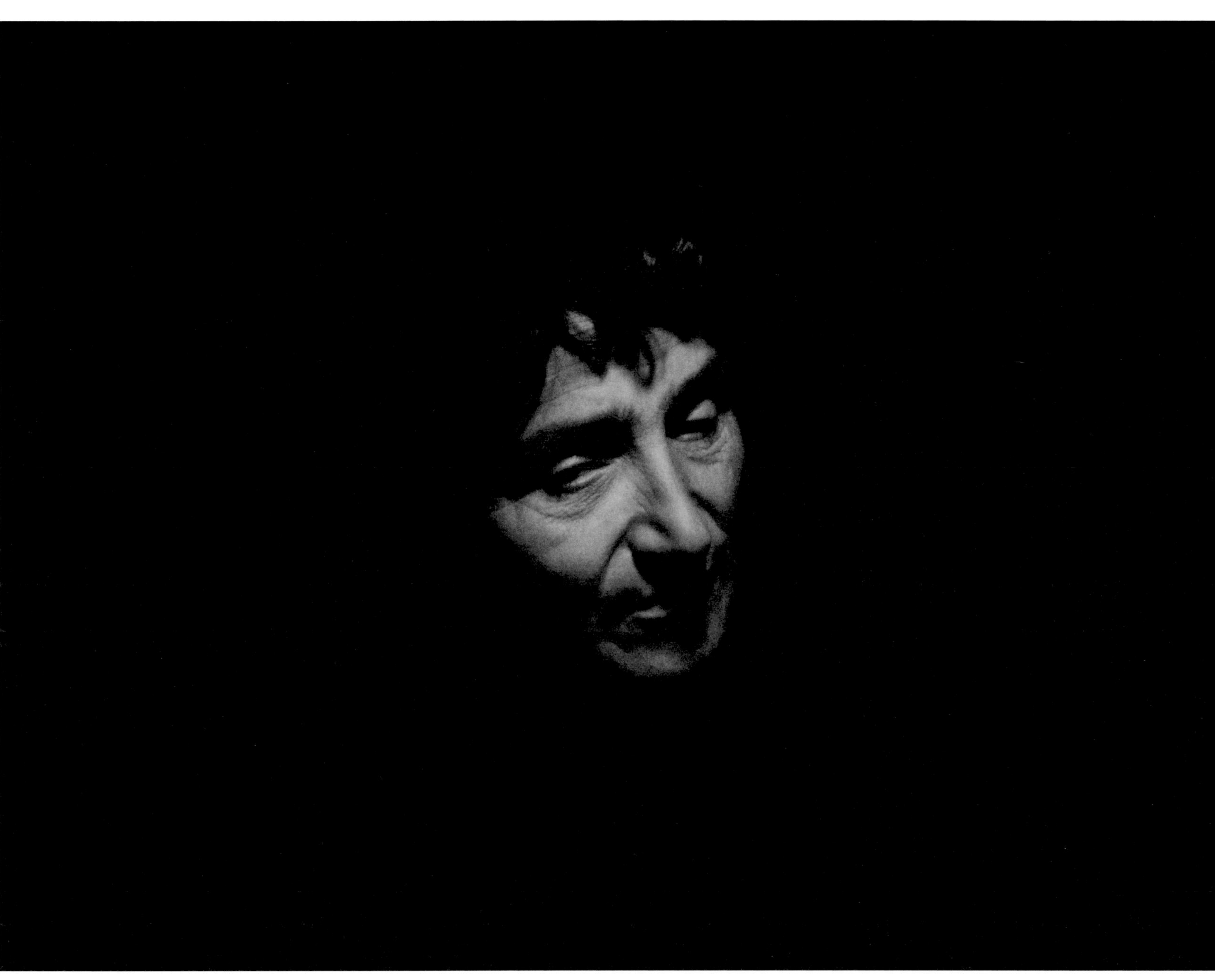

PERSONA 1015195

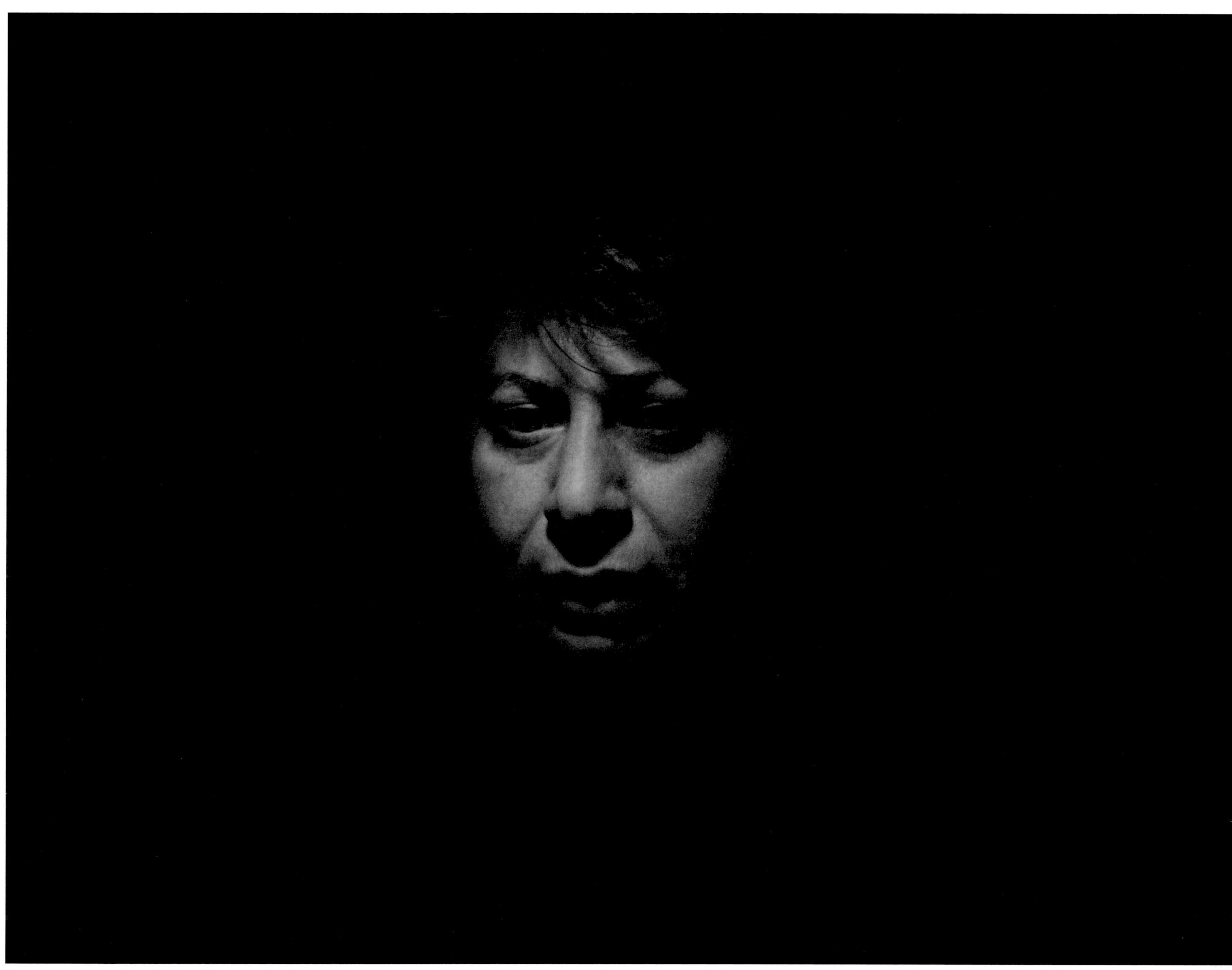

PERSONA 1019188

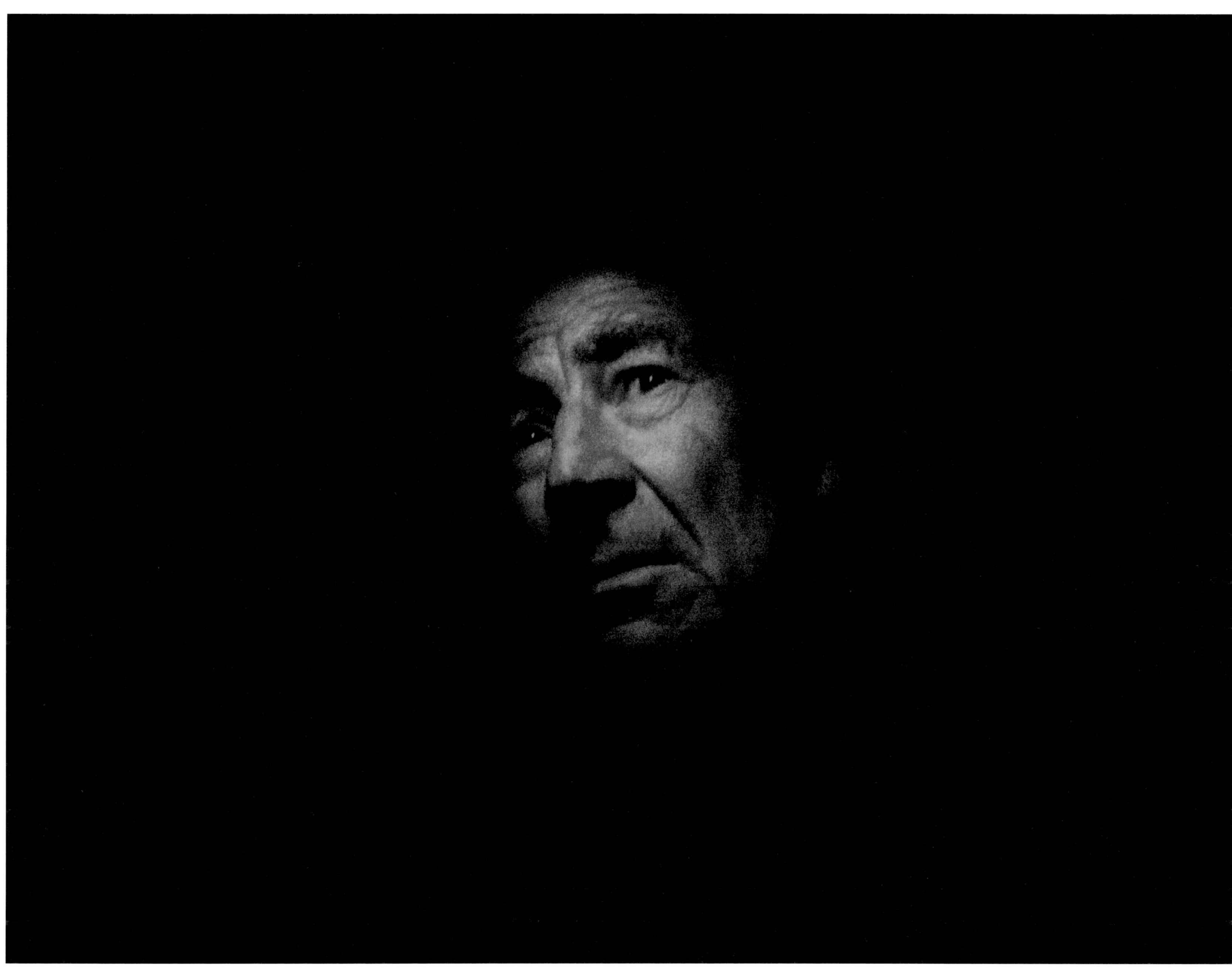

PERSONA 1019715

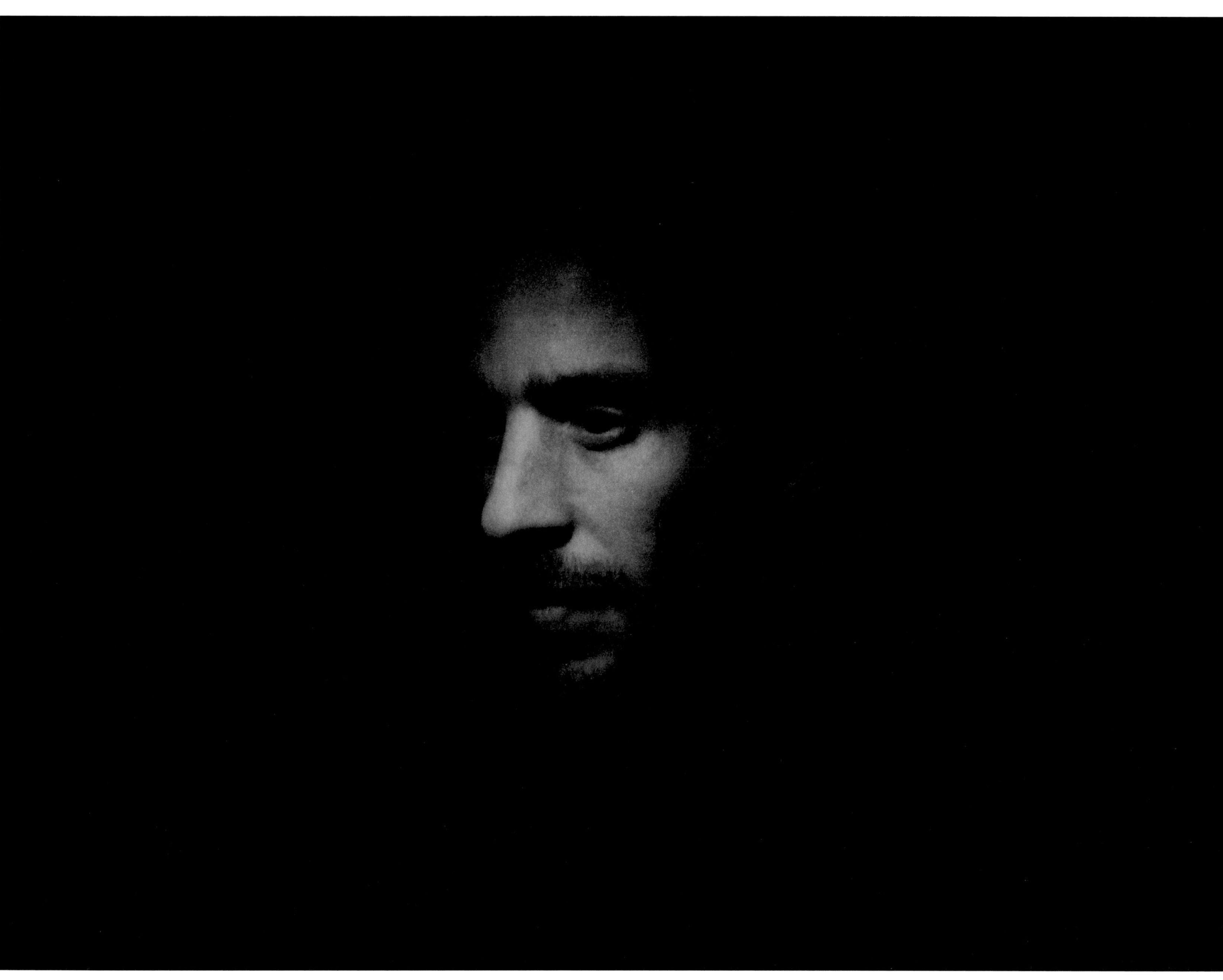

PERSONA 1015222

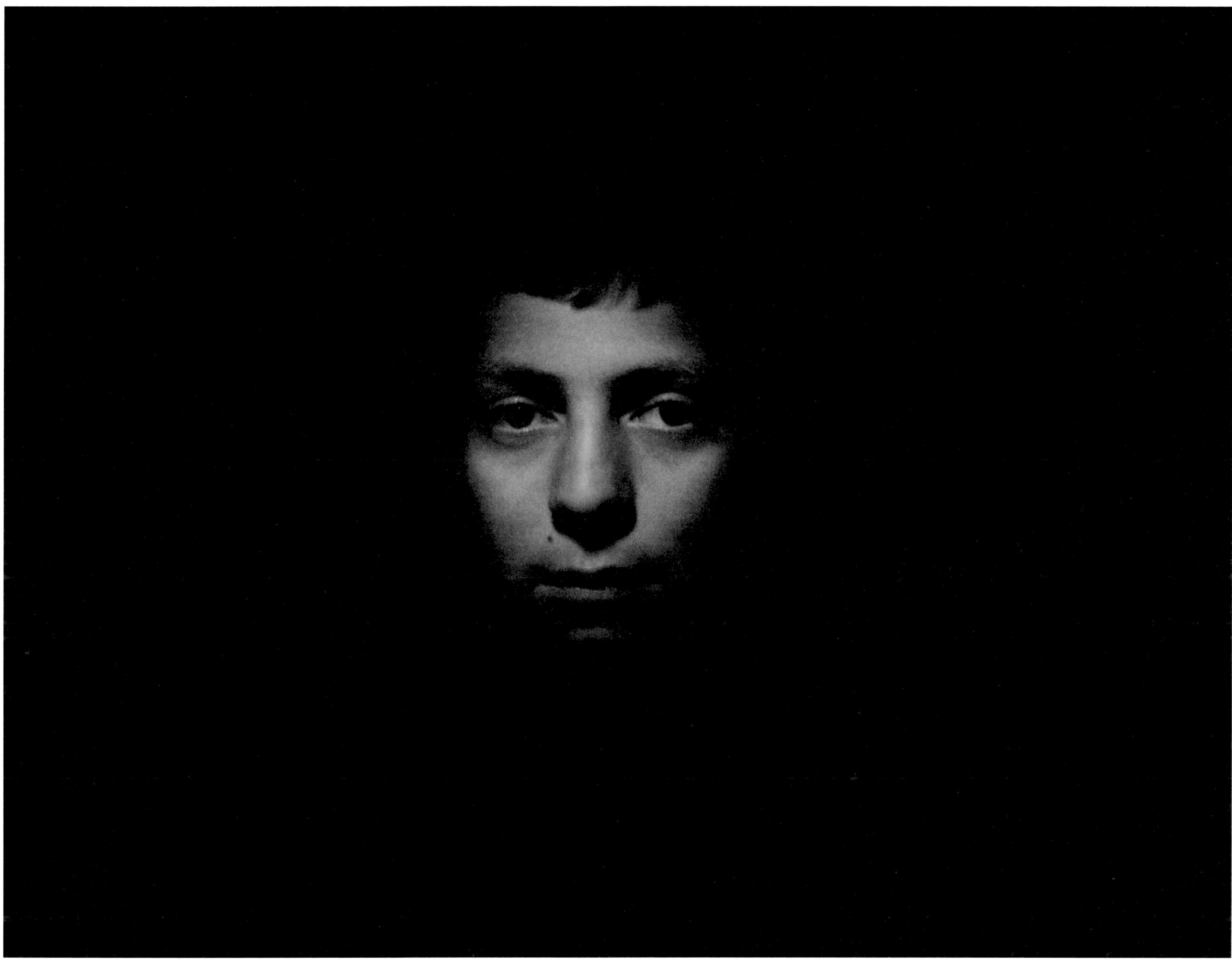

PERSONA 9092449

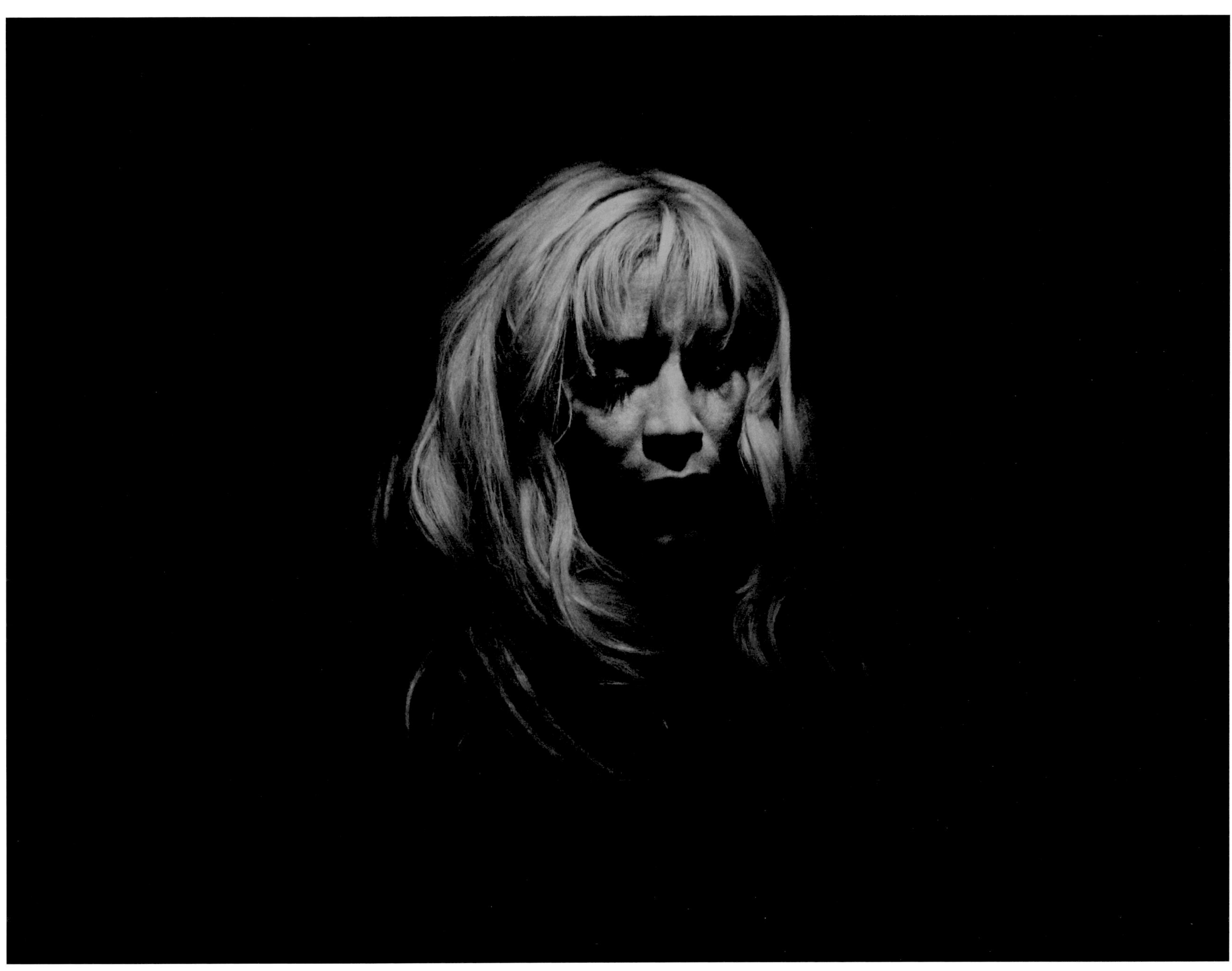

PERSONA 1019429

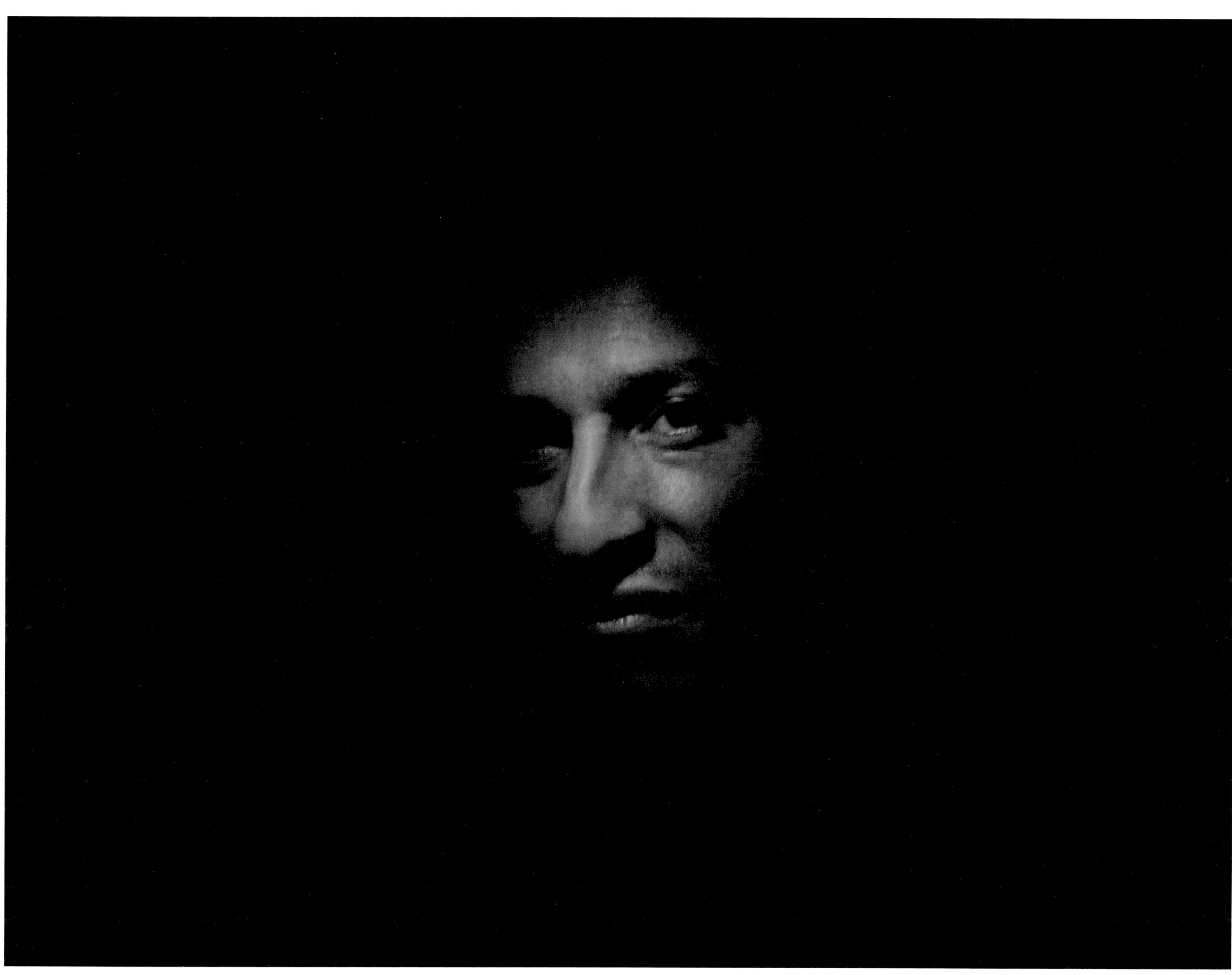

PERSONA 1018143

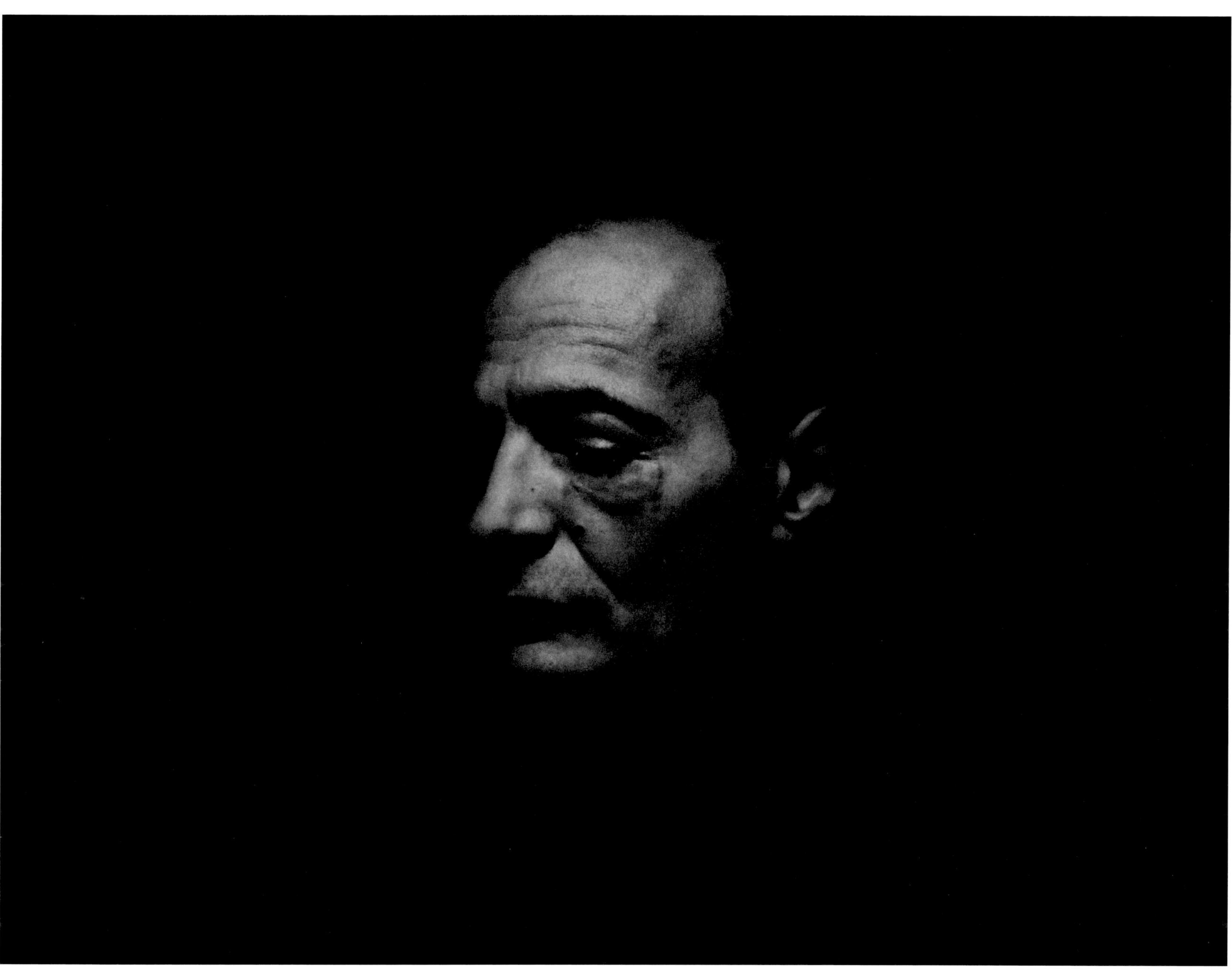

PERSONA 1014538

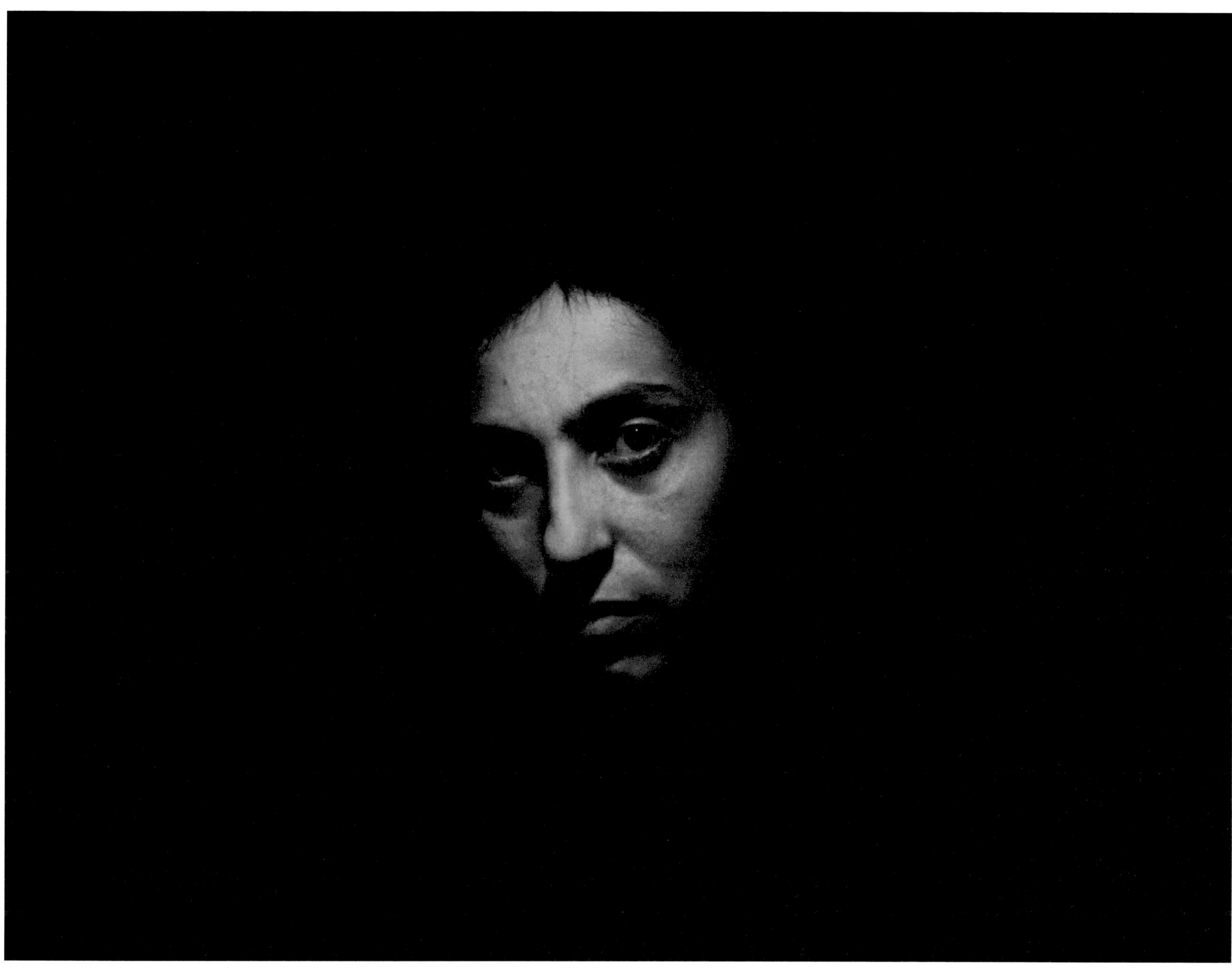

PERSONA 1019221

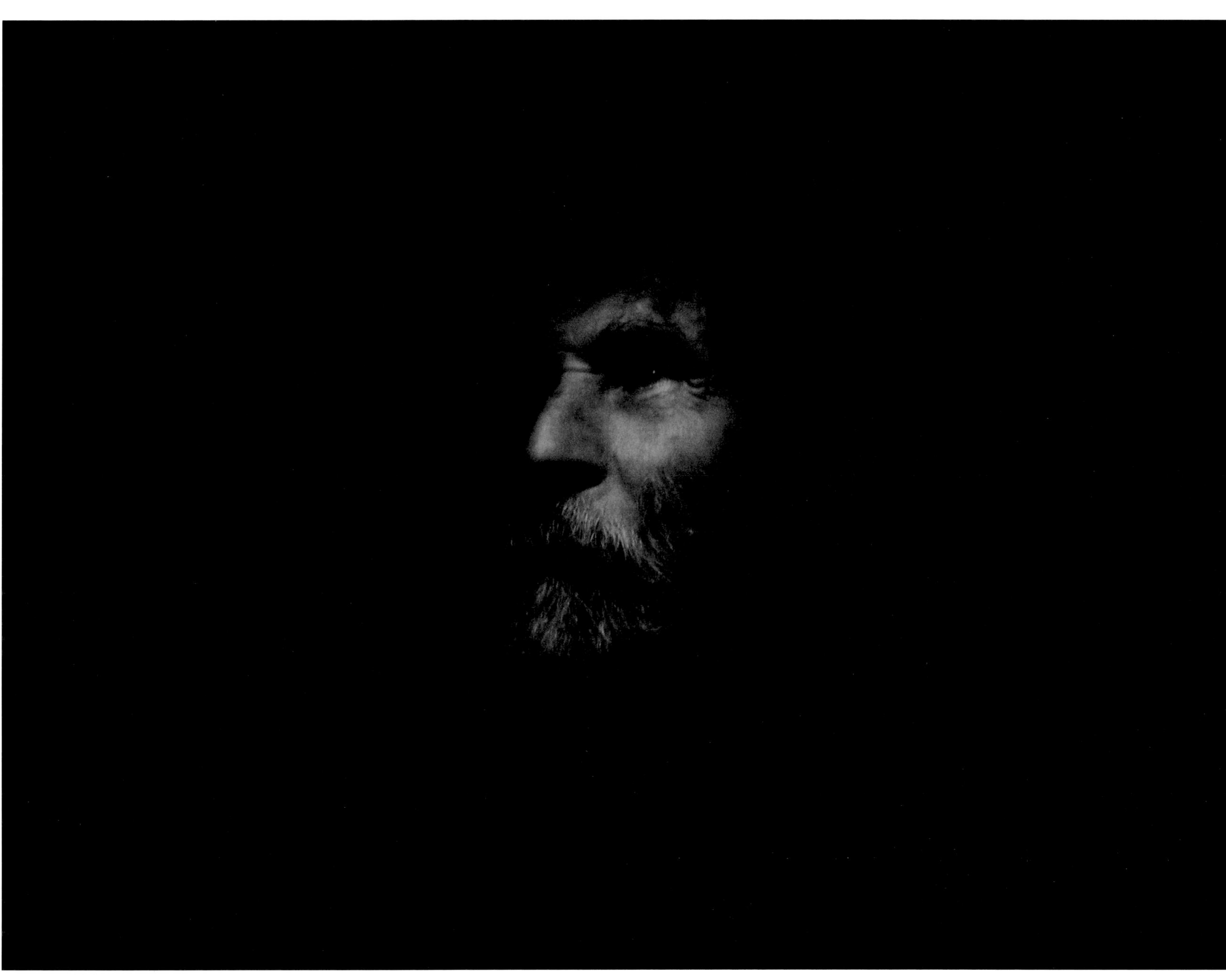

PERSONA 1018213

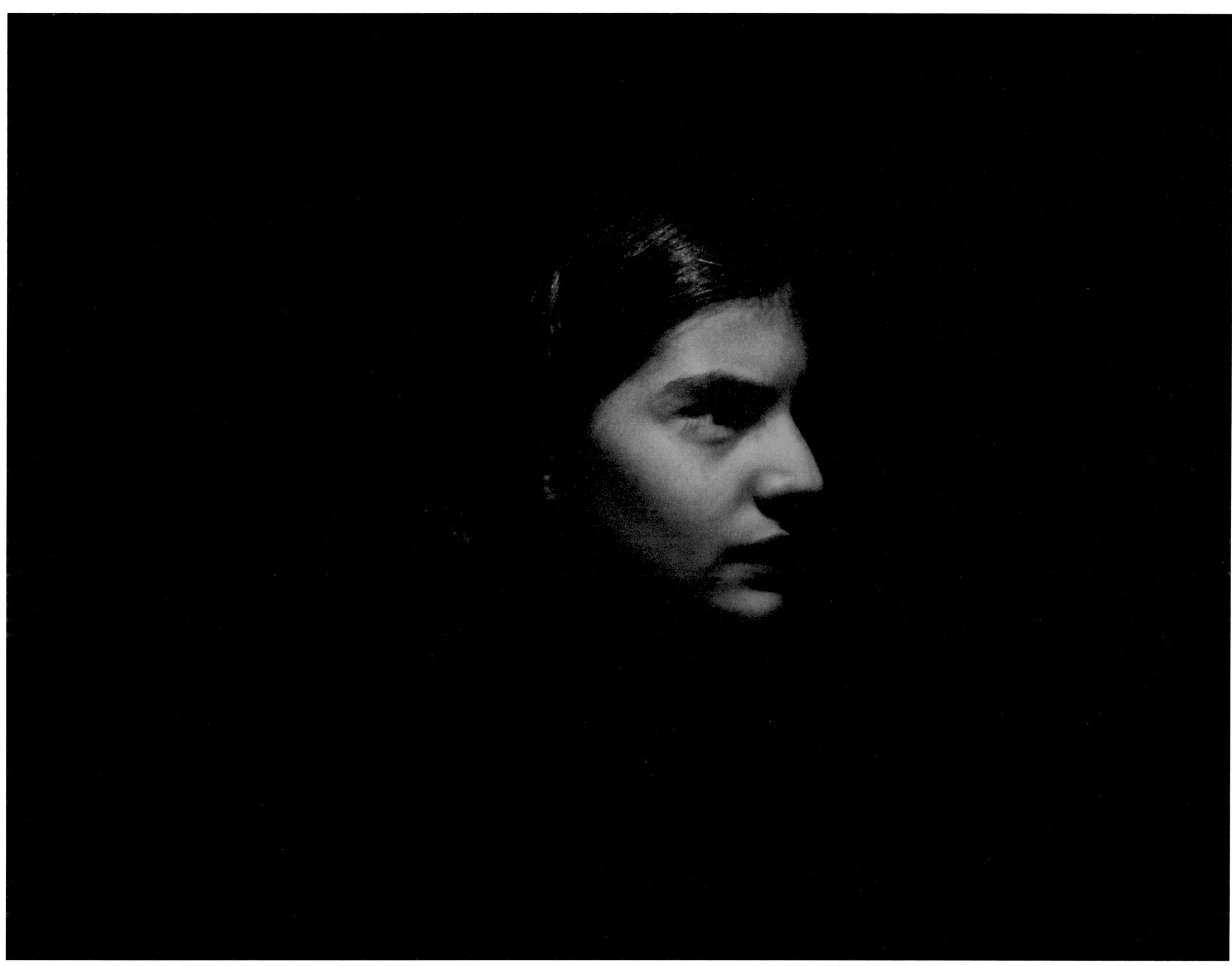

PERSONA 1011843

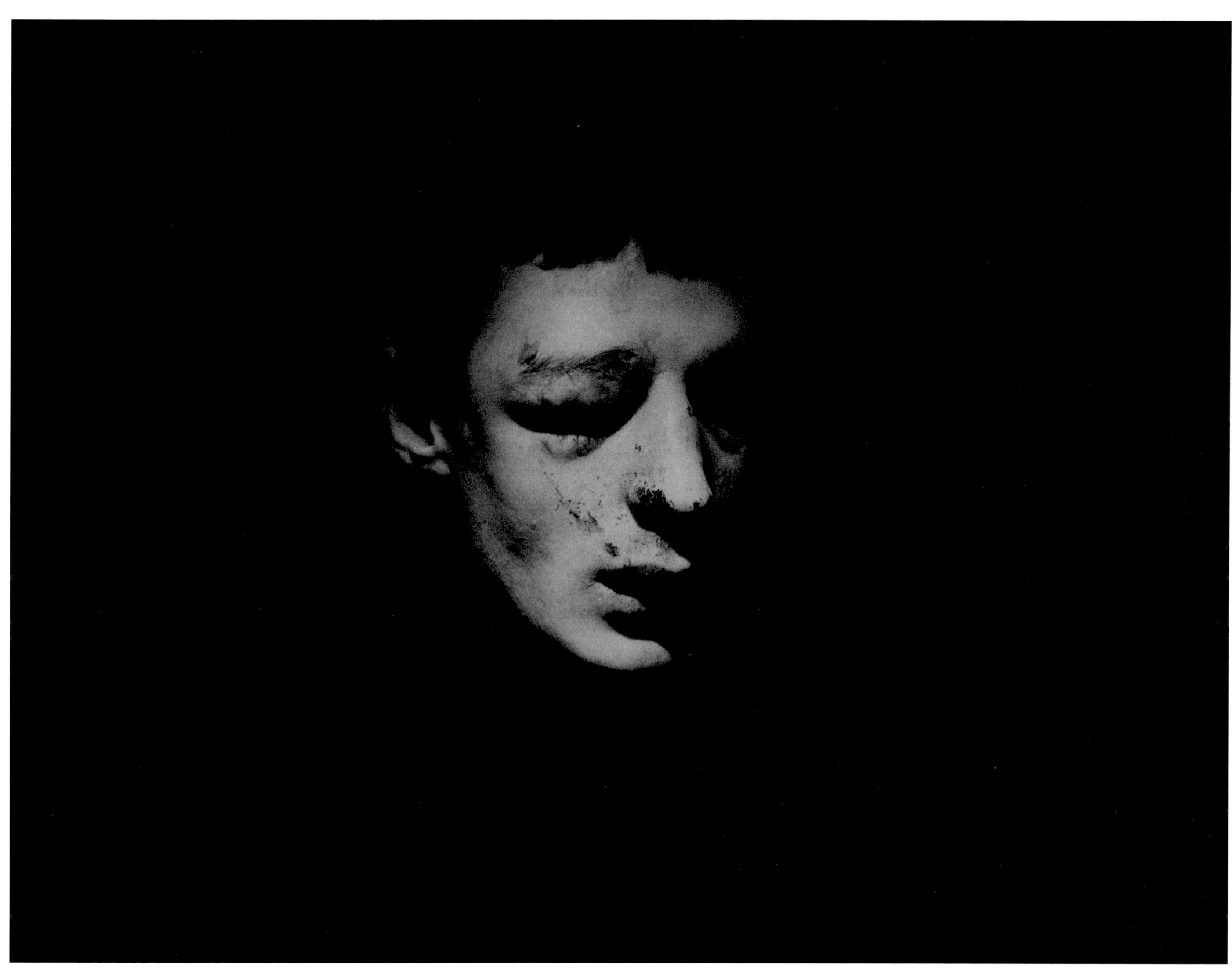

PERSONA 1018203

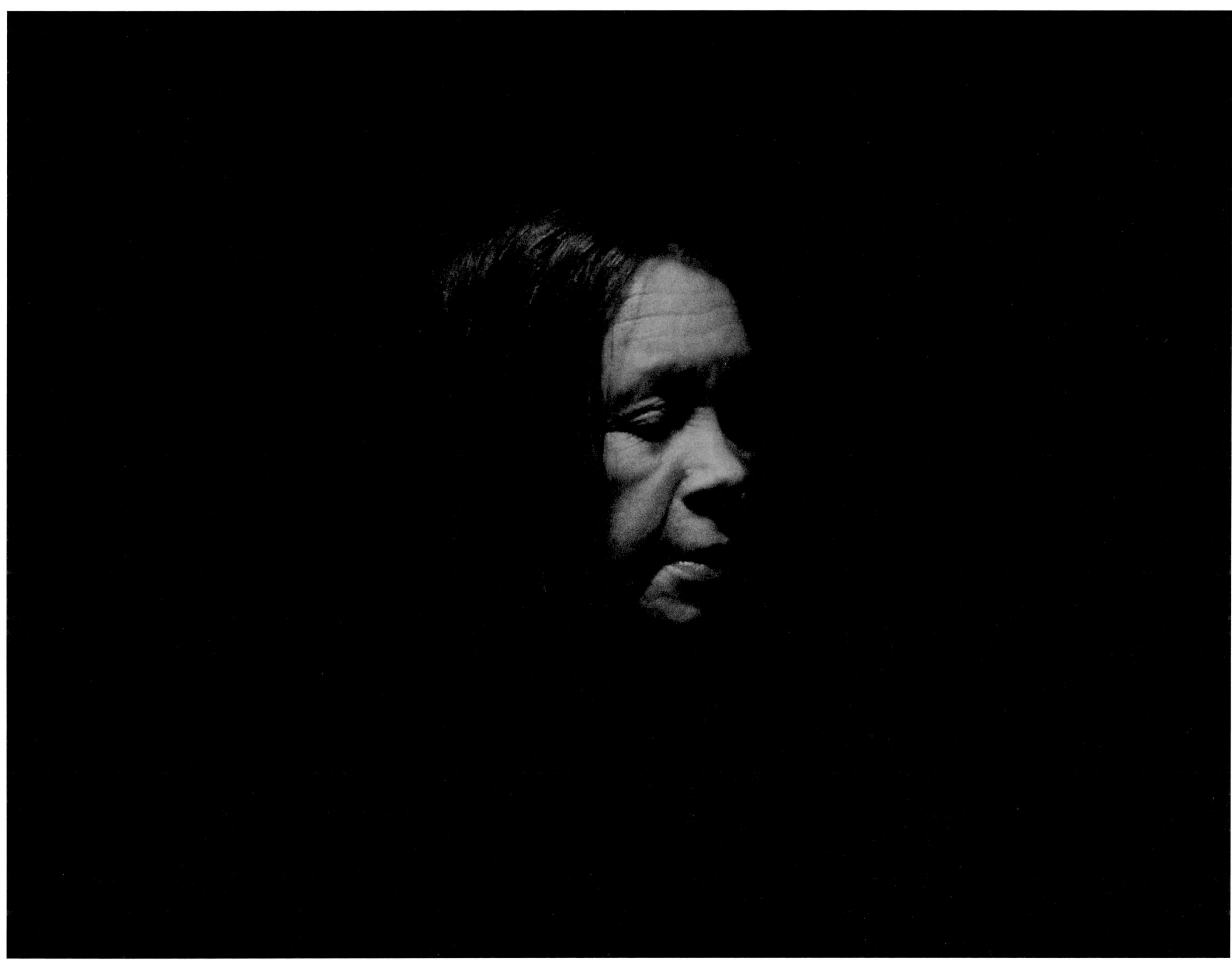

PERSONA 1015149

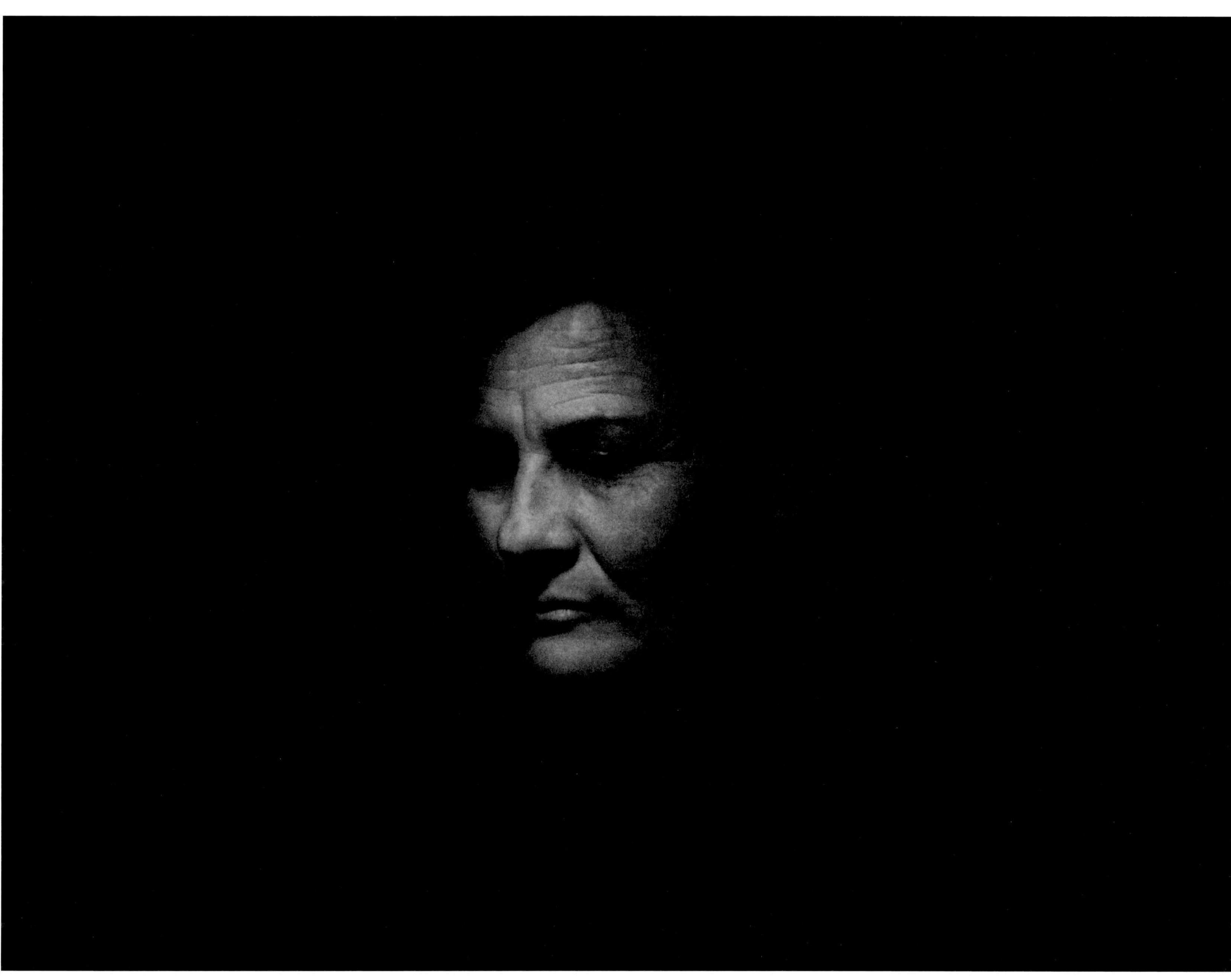

PERSONA 1019604

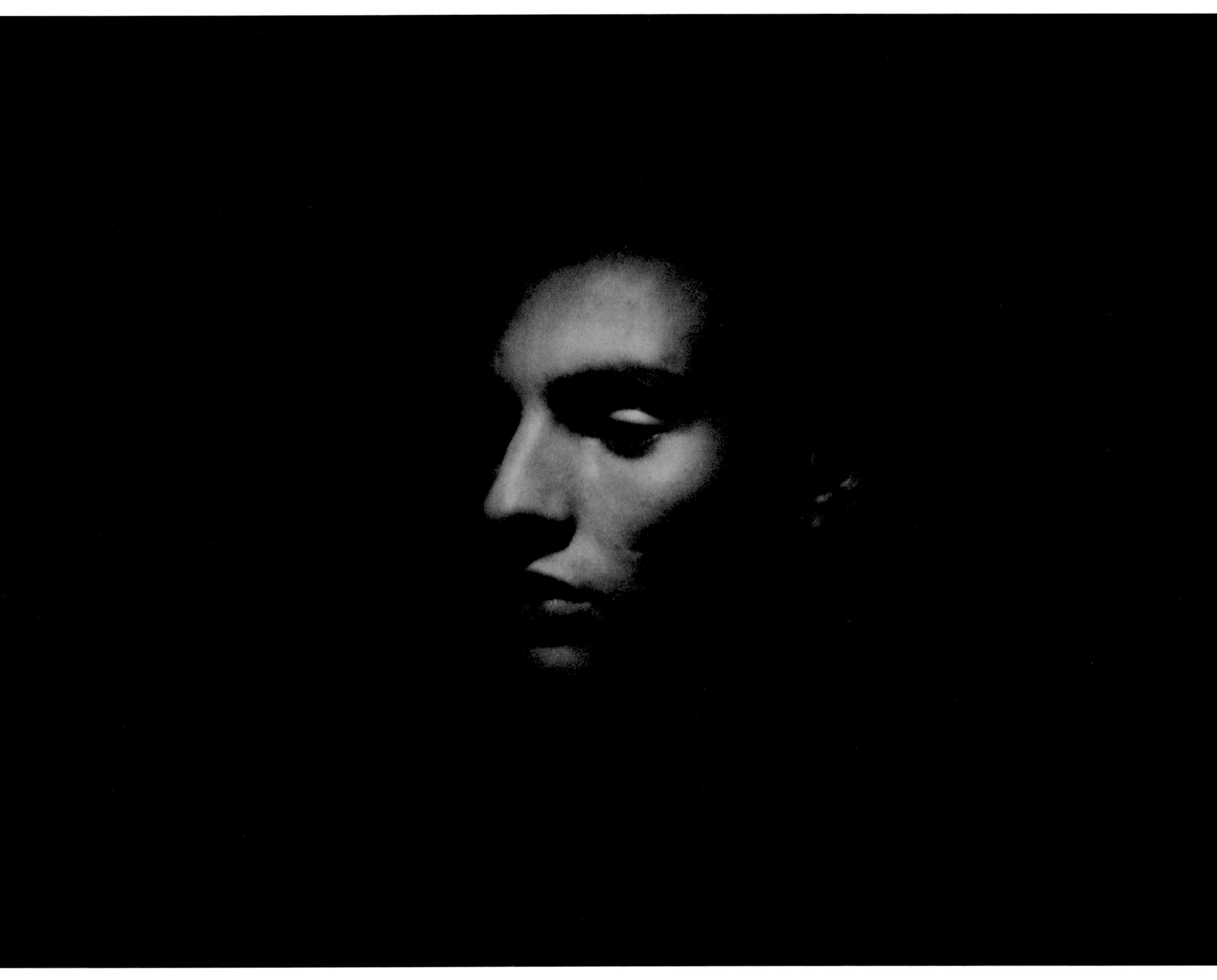

PERSONA 1019731

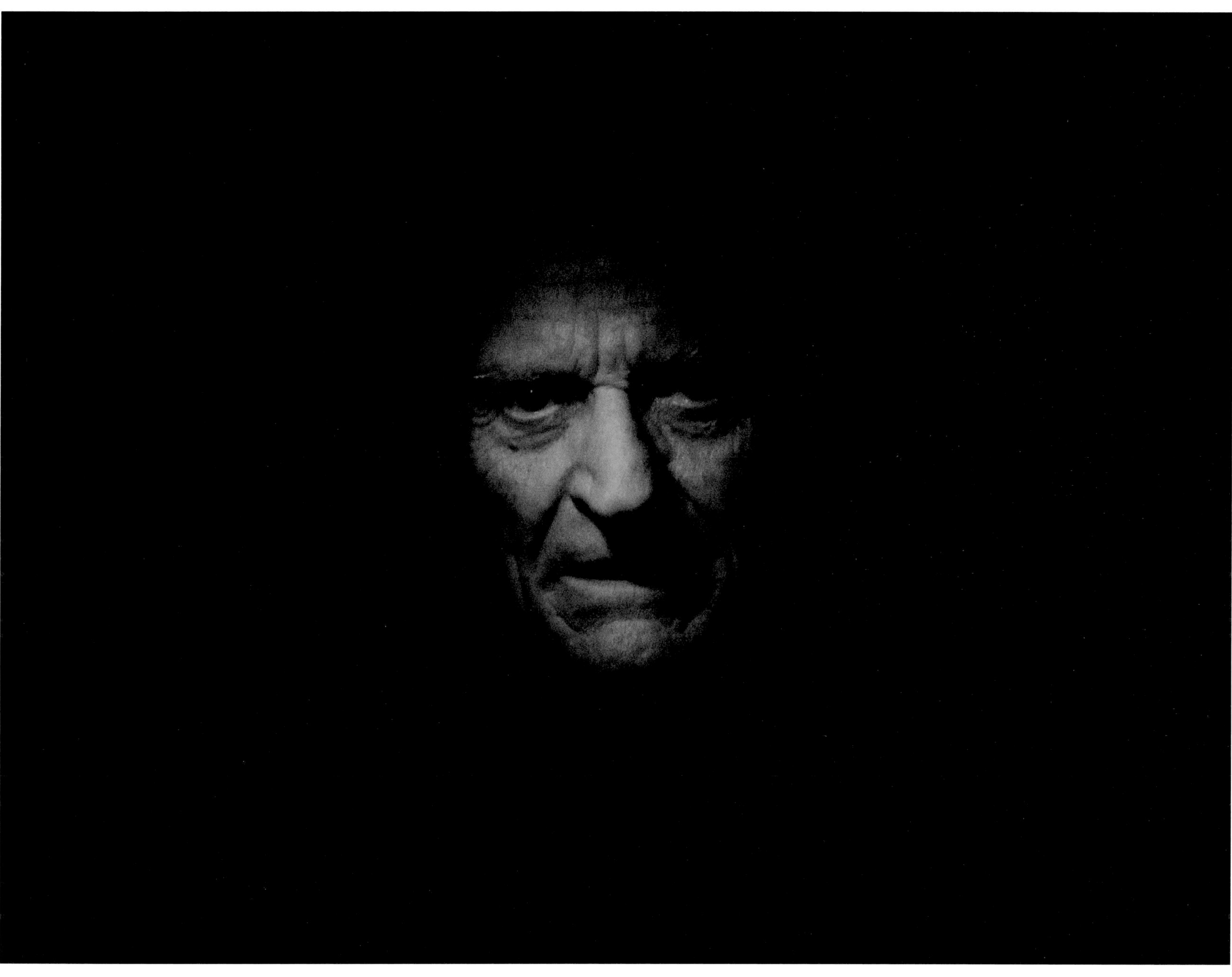

EXCERPTS

FROM "SIX CHARACTERS IN SEARCH OF AN AUTHOR"
by Luigi Pirandello

"A character, sir, can always ask a man who he is. Because a character really has his own life, marked with his own characteristics, by virtue of which he is always someone. Whereas a man – I am not speaking of you now – a man can be no one."
"Perform this!"
"But you don't. You don't express. You provide us with raw material. The actors give it body and face, voice and gesture. They've given expression to much loftier material, let me tell you. Yours is on such a small scale that, if it stands up on stage at all, the credit, believe me, should go to my actors."
"Oh, for Heaven's sake! Here the actors act you, and that's that!"
"I'll know how to live it too, don't worry, once I put myself in the role!"
"He had the good luck to die."
"Story is right! Fiction! Literature!"
"Literature? This is life, sir. Passion!"
"For will not all that you feel yourself to be now, your whole reality of today, as it is now, inevitably seem an illusion tomorrow?"
"But ours does not, sir. You see, that is the difference. It does not change, it cannot ever change or be otherwise because it is already fixed, it is what is, just that, forever – a terrible thing, sir! – an immutable reality."
"The drama is inside us. It is us."

FROM "THE BOOK OF HOURS: LOVE POEMS TO GOD"
by Rainer Maria Rilke

NO ONE LIVES HIS LIFE

Disguised since childhood,
haphazardly assembled
from voices and fears
and little pleasures,

We come of age as masks.
Our true face never speaks.

Somewhere there must be storehouses
where all these lives are laid away
like suits of armor or old carriages
or clothes hanging limply on the walls.

Maybe all paths lead there,
to the repository of unlived things.

All images have been taken with Olympus cameras.

ACKNOWLEDGMENTS

Special thanks to Daria Birang for her invaluable support, Alessandro Sala for post-production and being super assistant, Luca Santese for assisting in post-production, Lorenza Orlando, Francois Pinassaud and Cesuralab for their hard work on this project.
For their precious opinions and friendship:
Daria Birang, Luc Delahaye, Diane Dufur, Gilles Peress, Chris Anderson, Jonathan Frantini, Gigi Giannuzzi, Melissa Harris, Chris Boot, Quentin Bajac, Alec Soth, Antoine D'Agata and Adrian Kelterborn.
For their hospitality and valued contributions:
Soraya Amrane, Lucille Lagier, Coskun Asar, Jacqueline Blanc, Brigitte Colnot, Zane Jacobs, Sandro Ozbetelashvili, Kakha Tolordava, Thomas Dworzak.

PUBLISHED IN GREAT BRITAIN IN 2010 BY TROLLEY LTD
www.trolleybooks.com

Photographs © Alex Majoli 2010

The right of Alex Majoli to be identified as the author of this work has been asserted by him in accordance with the copyright, designs and patents act 1998.

A catalogue record for this book is available from the British Library.

ISBN 978-1-907112-22-5